WHAT Is the largest sea structure built by animals?

Om KIDZ
An imprint of Om Books International

Contents

What is a sea?

A large body of saline water! A sea is a body of saline water that is surrounded completely or partly by land. The sea moderates the Earth's climate and plays an important role in controlling the flow of water on Earth, by the process of water cycle. Seas are also home to many animals.

Pocket fact

Echo sounder!
The depth of sea is measured using a device called Depth Finder, also known as Echo Sounder. It is done by measuring the time taken for a sound (sonic pulse) produced just below the water surface to return, or echo, from the bottom of the water body.

Find out

What does "Pacific" mean?

What is the maximum depth of the ocean?

It's approximately 11,000 metres! The depth of the ocean is often said to begin at the edge of the continental shelf. However, if depth is measured from the ocean floor, the Challenger Deep in the Pacific Ocean is the deepest point on Earth. It measures nearly 11 kilometers below the ocean.

What makes an ocean different from a sea?

Its size! Oceans are vast water bodies that cover approximately 70% of the Earth, whereas seas are smaller compared to oceans. Oceans are bounded by the continents, or the equator, and other imaginary lines. On the other hand, seas are usually surrounded by land on all or most sides. Seas are also believed to lack a natural outlet.

Find out

What are algae? Are they found only in oceans?

Pocket fact

It's so large!

The largest ocean in the world is the Pacific Ocean. It covers a length of approximately 60,060,700 square miles.The largest sea in the world is the Mediterranean Sea that covers an area of 970,000 square miles.

What lies under an ocean?

There are many aquatic animals, some plants and other structures! Oceans and seas are home to rich and diverse marine life. Lobsters and crabs live in shallow waters. In deeper water, we can find many types of fish, dolphins and whales. Plants, such as sea grass grow in the ocean. You can also find minerals, pearls, coral reefs, algae and precious stones in the ocean.

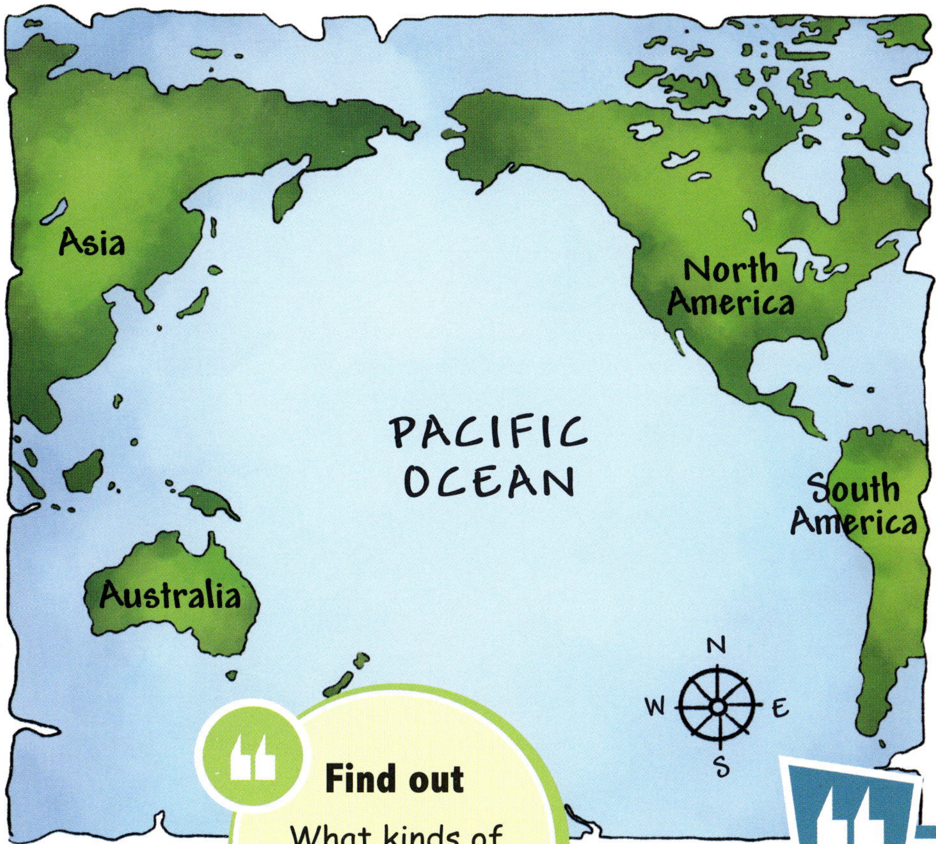

What is ocean floor?

The bottom of the ocean is called the ocean floor. The ocean floor has mountains, volcanoes and deep trenches just like the land. Canyons, abysses and slopes make up the landscape of the ocean floor. The sunlight, and its warmth, fades away as you go deeper into the ocean. Due to the lack of sunlight, most of the ocean floor is lifeless.

Find out

What kinds of animals live in the Mesopelagic zone?

Pocket fact

The largest mountain range!
The Mid-Ocean Ridge is the largest mountain range on Earth. It exists beneath the ocean and stretches up to 40,389 miles. It is located on the boundaries of multiple tectonic plates.

What are the three main zones of the ocean?

They are the Epipelagic, Mesopelagic and Bathypelagic zones! The ocean is divided into three zones, based on the amount of sunlight that penetrates the ocean waters. The Epipelagic zone is the sunlight zone because it receives enough sunlight to support photosynthesis. The next zone is the Mesopelagic zone that receives some sunlight but it is not enough for photosynthesis to occur. The last zone is the Bathypelagic zone that receives no sunlight. This zone can reach depths of almost 20,000 feet.

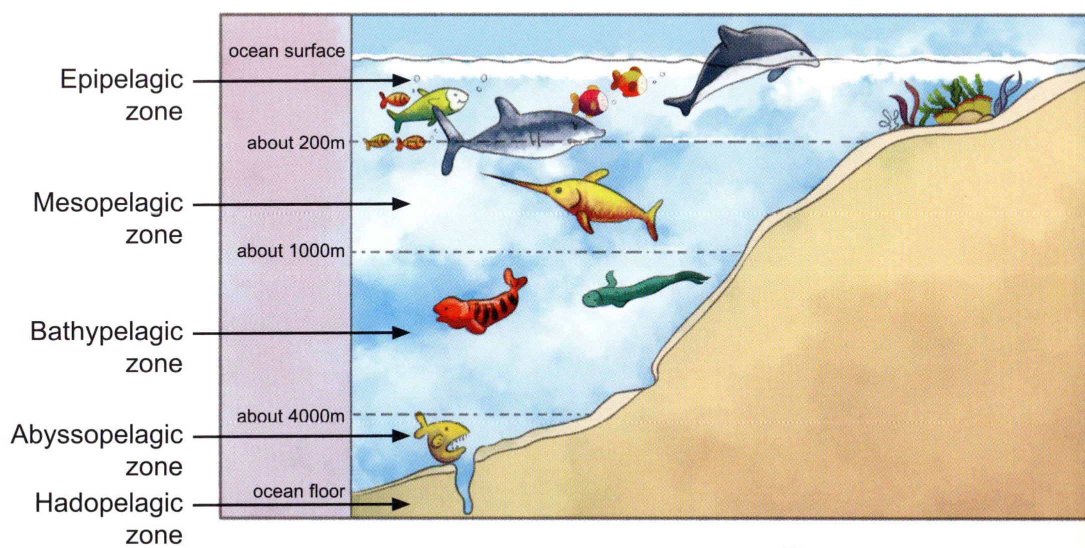

What's the deepest ocean in the world?

It's the Pacific Ocean! The Pacific Ocean extends from the Arctic Ocean in the north to the Southern Ocean in the south. It is bounded by Asia and Australia in the west and the Americas in the east. It is not only the largest but also the deepest ocean on Earth. It has an average depth of around 11,000 feet.

Find out

What is the length of the Ring of Fire?

Pocket fact

The Ring of Fire!
75% of the world's active and dormant volcanoes are found in the Pacific Ocean. This area is called the Ring of Fire, an area in the basin of the Pacific Ocean.

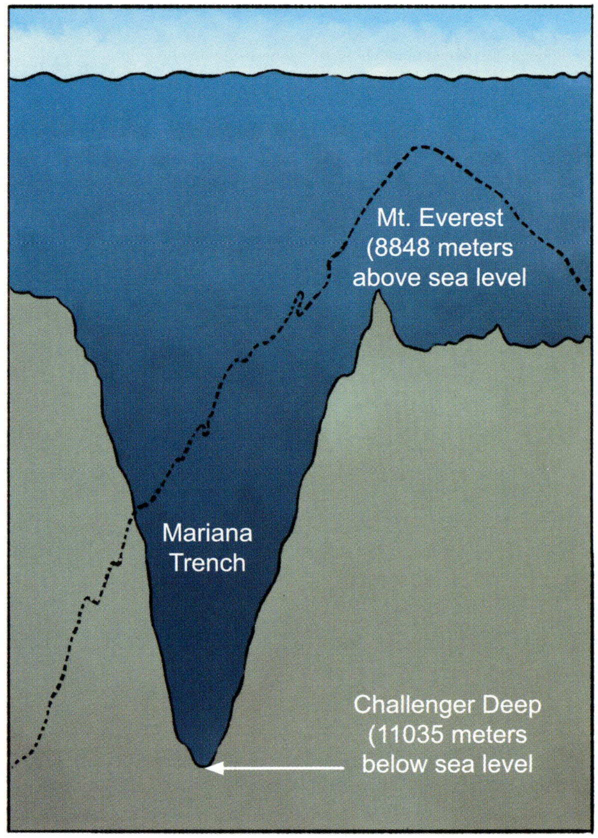

What's the deepest part of the Earth's oceans?

It's the Mariana Trench! It is located in the western Pacific Ocean, approximately 200 kilometres to the east of the Mariana Islands, in the Western Pacific East of Philippines. The depths of the Mariana Trench were first measured in 1875 by the British ship H.M.S. Challenger, as part of the first global oceanographic cruise. Its deepest point, the Challenger Deep, was first explored by Jacques Piccard and Navy Lt. Don Wash in 1960. After a five-hour long descent, they could only spend 20 minutes there!

What causes waves on the surface of seas and oceans?

The action of the wind! Surface waves or wind-driven waves are created by the friction between wind and surface water. As the wind blows across the surface of the ocean or lake, it transfers some energy to the water. This continuous disturbance creates a wave. Stronger winds like storm surges cause larger waves.

Pocket fact

That's high!
The world's highest tides are formed at the Bay of Fundy on the Atlantic Coast of North America. During some times of the year the difference between high tide and low tide is around 53 feet and 6 inches, which is equivalent to a five-storey building.

Find out

What do we call waves that transmit energy from the sea area across the ocean?

What are tides?

The rise and fall in the levels of the ocean! Tides are very long-period waves that move through the ocean and are caused by the gravitational pull of the moon. When the moon is closer to one side of the Earth, it pulls the ocean water towards it. The ocean water rises and the waves are closer to the banks. This is called high tide. Meanwhile, the water levels go down at the other part of the Earth, which is farther from the moon, thus forming a low tide.

What are rip currents?

A rip current is a strong current of water running from a beach back to the ocean. It is formed in gaps between sandbars, piers or parts of a reef. Sometimes when heavy waves break on the shore, these underwater obstacles (like sandbars) block the waves from washing directly back to the sea. The wave then runs along the shore until it finds an opening around the obstacle. It rushes to the opening, just like water rushes down a drain and creates a rip current.

Find out

At what speed do rip currents move?

Pocket fact

Wave Train!

Wave Train refers to a group of waves that have similar or equal wavelengths and travel in the same direction. The time period between these waves is called the "wave period".

What is a Tsunami?

Tsunamis are huge waves caused by earthquakes or volcanic eruptions under the ocean. When an earthquake occurs under the ocean floor, a huge amount of energy is transferred to the water above it. This creates a very long, high sea wave called Tsunami. The word Tsunami comes from the Japanese words tsu (harbour) and nami (wave).

What makes oceans look green sometimes?

The presence of algae and phytoplankton! Phytoplankton are microscopic marine plants that carry out photosynthesis with the help of chlorophyll and other light-harvesting pigments. Chlorophyll absorbs sunlight and reflects green light. Ocean water appears green at some places due to the presence of high concentrations of phytoplankton.

Try this!

Imagine that you have dived into the bottom of the ocean. Narrate your experience.

Pocket fact

Radio signals help!
Information about the world's oceans and seas, such as their colour, height of waves, temperature and so on are gathered by satellites and sent back via radio signals to the Earth.

What keeps the ocean from draining through the sand?

Have you ever noticed that water runs through sand? If there is sand at the bottom of the ocean why doesn't all the water in the ocean drain out of it? This is because the ocean floor is not completely made of sand. It consists of many materials, such as thicker soils and sediments. The deepest parts of the ocean are made up of rocks and minerals that hold the water in the world's oceans.

What is sea glass?

Sea glass refers to the beautiful, smooth pieces of glass found on the beaches along the oceans and seas. It is made of glass trash that comes from broken bottles, jars and glassware. When pieces of glass are thrown around by the sea, they break and are tossed around by the waves. After many years all the sharp edges and corners of these pieces become smooth, forming sea glass.

Find out

What is the tallest iceberg?

Pocket fact

Mermaid tears!

Sea glass is known by several names which include sea gems, beach jewels, mermaid's tears and sea pearls.

What is an iceberg?

Icebergs are large masses of ice floating in open water! They usually break-off from glaciers or ice shelves. Not all chunks of ice are called icebergs. Huge pieces that extend out of the water by at least 17 feet and are 50-feet long are called icebergs.

What are marine habitats?

They are aquatic habitats which contain salt water! Marine habitats include oceans, lakes, seas, rocky and sandy shores, tide-pools, estuaries and salt marshes. These habitats are home to seaweeds, algae, sea grass, fish, sea mammals, sea birds, coral, jellyfish and other marine creatures.

Find out

Are sea anemones plants or animals?

Pocket fact

Seas and oceans are home to many crustaceans, such as crabs, shrimp and lobsters. Crustaceans are animals which have strong skeletons outside their body. These skeletons are made of calcium.

What kind of plants grow in the ocean?

Phytoplankton, algae, kelp, sea grass and many others! The most common plants found in the ocean are Phytoplankton. They are single-celled plants that float freely on the surface of water. Sea grasses are marine plants with roots that live on the ocean floor. These flowering plants are the habitat of small fish and other marine life.

What is the fastest creature in the ocean?

It's the sailfish! The sailfish is a well-known species of fish that can be recognized by its large dorsal fin. The fin looks like a sail that has accordion pleats. It is considered the fastest marine creature and can move at 68 miles per hour!

Find out

What are kelp forests?

Pocket fact

The smallest!

The smallest fish in the sea is the Stout infantfish. It lives in the Great Barrier Reef in Australia.

What is the fastest growing plant in the ocean?

It's the Giant kelp! The Giant kelp is a species of large seaweed that is found in the eastern Pacific, as well as southern South America, South Africa and Australia. It can grow up to 2 feet per day. Under suitable conditions, the Giant kelp can also grow to a length of more than 100 feet in a little more than a year; and attain a maximum height of around 200 feet.

What makes sea otters special?

They don't have blubber; they use tools and lots more! Sea otters live in shallow coastal waters in the Pacific Ocean. They can dive up to 330 feet in search of food. They are the only marine mammals that don't have the layer of fat called blubber. They hold hands while sleeping to ensure that they do not drift apart. Interestingly, sea otters also use "tools" such as a rock to open their hard-shelled prey!

Pocket fact

I was born in water!
Sea otter is the only otter that gives birth in the water. The mother otter nurtures its young ones while floating on its back. It holds the infants on its chest to nurse them, and quickly teaches them to swim and hunt.

Find out

Where do sea otters hide the rocks they collect?

What do sea otters eat?

Sea otters feed on hard-shelled sea animals. They eat mussels, urchins, abalone, crabs, snails, clams and other marine species. After eating, they wash themselves in the ocean and clean their coat with their teeth and paws!

What are corals?

Corals are sea animals without a backbone. They belong to a large group of colourful and fascinating animals called Cnidaria. They have a single mouth opening surrounded by stinging tentacles. Each coral animal is called a polyp. Most of the polyps live in groups of hundreds to thousands and form a "colony".

Find out

What are soft corals?

Pocket fact

World Heritage Site!
The Great Barrier Reef is recognised as one of the seven natural wonders of the world. It was named a UNESCO World Heritage site in 1981.

What is the largest sea structure built by animals?

It's the Great Barrier Reef! The Great Barrier Reef is a coral reef system located in the Coral Sea, off the coast of Queensland, Australia. It extends for more than 2,000 kilometres and has an area of around 350,000 square kilometres. It is said to be the largest structure ever built by living creatures!

What is a beach?

A beach is a narrow strip of land that lies along the edge of an ocean, or sea. It separates the water body from the inland areas. A beach is usually made of sand, tiny particles of rocks and minerals that have been worn down by the action of wind and waves.

Pocket fact

Longest beach!
The Praia do Cassino located in Brazil is the longest beach in the world; it is over 150 miles in length.

Find out

Which animals are commonly found on the coast?

What is a coast?

The coast is a broad area of land that borders the sea. It is also known as a shore. The coast may be made up of different landforms, such as beaches, cliffs, headlines, etc. The boundary of a coast, where land meets water, is called the coastline. The way coasts are formed depends a lot on what kind of material is present in the land and water.

Index